WAHOO SUNSET

ALSO BY SCOTT KEENEY

Above the Surface (with Rachel Archelaus)

Early Returns

Pickpocket Poetica

Sappho Does Hay(na)ku

Walloping Shrug

WAHOO SUNSET

POEMS

Scott Keeney

SOME CLOUDS PRESS

Copyright © 2019 Scott Keeney

This book contains a found poem, a traditional poetry form, not plagiarism. Directly pointing it out would lessen the fun.

Cover art by Rachel Archelaus
Book design by Scott Keeney
Typeset in Dante MT

ISBN 978-1-948728-06-5 (paperback)
ISBN 978-1-948728-05-8 (ebook)

CONTENTS

Acknowledgments ix

Without Which No Art 1

Sleep Backwards Peels 2

The Year of the Rabbit 3

On Meeting Robert Creeley 7

Swinging Lullaby 9

Concupiscent Fire 11

On Meeting John Ashbery 13

Nonchalance Terminal 15

Impatient Forever 16

Apterous Dragonfly 17

Gravitational Hum 19

On Meeting Charles Wright 20

What I Wanted To Say Before 21

Chance Works 23

On Meeting Elizabeth Bishop 25

Everyday Masterpiece 27

Dear Reader 29

Meditative Chatter 30

On Meeting Gregory Corso 33

To See the with the Far Removed and Sing 34

Metaphysical Skill Set 35

On Meeting Charles Simic   37

The Proletariat's End   39

Another Day Comes Hither   40

On Meeting Elaine Equi   41

Cognitive Slog   43

Unmendable Guitar String Theory   44

On Meeting Allen Ginsberg   45

Mysterious Shibboleth   47

Mysterious Opponents   48

Cambial Mirror   49

On Meeting Donald Hall   50

Changeling Complex   51

Gung-Ho Contingency Plan   53

Night Song   54

Hellacious Evergreen   55

Greater Than Gone   56

On Meeting Louise Glück   57

Only Air   59

The Articulated Bridge of Now   60

Nightbroke   61

Phenomenological Dexterity   62

On Meeting Ted Berrigan   64

Wahoo Sunset   65

Standing in a Corner of the Sky   67

In the Middle of the Sea
a Mirror on the Wall   68

In the Middle of the Mirror
a Sea on the Wall   69

A Poem for Despisers of Poetry   70

On Meeting Bill Knott   71

Ineffable More   72

Video Glass   73

How To Collage   75

Luminous Hush   76

Down with Matter   77

The Day Before New Year's Eve   79

As Long As Grubs Blossom   80

On Meeting Aram Saroyan   82

Overbaked Wahoo   83

To Frank O'Hara   84

Beginning To End   85

Nonstop Ending   86

Moon Shot   87

ACKNOWLEDGMENTS

My thanks to the editors of the publications in which the following poems first appeared, sometimes in different versions or under different titles.

AMP: "Phenomenological Dexterity" and "The Day Before New Year's Eve"

BlazeVOX: "Meditative Chatter" and "On Meeting Ted Berrigan"

Blue & Yellow Dog: "To See the with the Far Removed and Sing"

The Boiler: "Concupiscent Fire"

Columbia Poetry Review: "The Proletariat's End"

Court Green: "Without Which No Art"

E·ratio: "Video Glass"

Everyday Genius: "Apterous Dragonfly"

Failbetter: "On Meeting Charles Simic"; "On Meeting Charles Wright"; "On Meeting Elizabeth Bishop"; and "On Meeting John Ashbery"

Gobbet: "Metaphysical Skill Set"

The Helix: "On Meeting Donald Hall" and "On Meeting Gregory Corso"

Juked: "On Meeting Robert Creeley"

Mad Hatters' Review Blog: "Cambial Mirror"; "Gravitational Hum"; and "Hellacious Evergreen"

Mudlark: "Another Day Comes Hither"; "Chance Works"; "Cognitive Slog"; "Nonstop Ending"; "Swinging Lullaby"; and "Unmendable Guitar String Theory"

Otoliths: "Dear Reader"; "On Meeting Aram Saroyan"; and "Wahoo Sunset"

Scud: "Moon Shot"

Shampoo: "Sleep Backwards Peels"

Stirring: "Down with Matter"

Tinge: "The Year of the Rabbit"

UCity Review: "Gung-Ho Contingency Plan" and "What I Wanted To Say Before"

The heart of a man
is not as great as an amphitheater

                    TED BERRIGAN

WAHOO SUNSET

WITHOUT WHICH NO ART

Archaic clockwork, church bells ring
when this train rears its horn through town.
A mother puts on her wings of moss.
A daughter takes out her hurricane gown.

SLEEP BACKWARDS PEELS

and all sleep is backwards moving
as if walking backwards into
wakefulness and all sleep being
backward sleep peels away the rind
of day that builds itself up each
new day around the body heart
and mind the way a starling jaw

works with backward muscles to spring
the bill open rather than clamp
the bill shut so sleep is a springing
open and not a clamping shut
a peeling open of the fruit
of the day's labor the day's wide
forward-moving unawake work

THE YEAR OF THE RABBIT

That was the year I read only the major poets
like Jennifer Moxley, W. B. Keckler, and Lisa Jarnot.
I spent summer nights in the woods bare chested
inviting mosquito bites. I tried to work the lines
"Let me show you my thing/I am shaped like a heart"
into every poem I wrote as if it were indicative of
seer transformation. I limited my beverages to lemonade,
freshly squeezed, and water, and lost ten percent
of my body weight. I ate broccoli for the first time
at a Thai restaurant in New Haven with a friend
I saw for the last time. It smelled like a snare drum
with a hint of hi-hat. The friend was fine; she just
didn't like me anymore. "Whatever's Cool with Me"
played on the radio whenever I got emotional
and it made me feel like chamomile tea, which was
another beverage I permitted myself. When the leaves
fell from the trees that fall, I took the train into the City
to see Elaine Equi read at the Riverside Branch
of the New York Public Library. She talked about making
out with Jerome in the back row at poetry readings
and being asked to leave. I was sitting in the back row
with an old girlfriend. We didn't make out, but we liked
Elaine's story almost as much as we liked her poems,
and in the end we became boyfriend and girlfriend
again. The new millennium approached us like a twelve-
scoop ice cream sundae called The Challenge.
Prepositional phrases were out like galoshes
as it became clear the winter fashions were all about
lightning and ash, confrontation and fear. I shoveled
the walkway to get to my car and tweaked my back.

Out of work for a week, I read only the major poets
like Hoa Nguyen, Kevin Young, and John Olson.
I learned AppleScript and JavaScript and HTML.
When my back recovered I danced in my living room
like I was thirteen. I rode my stationary bike to
Faith No More and Rage Against the Machine.
I was inspired by Cornel West and Ralph Nader
more than Albert Gore. I entered parts of speech
into HyperCard with which I planned to compose
a revolutionary epic poem I expected no one
to actually read—it was all about the marketing—
but I got bored and called my girlfriend in Boston
every night to hear what was happening with her
creative writing degree. It was all metaphor and irony,
meter and consistency of tone, and fawning over
revision, the idea of it, with a dash of voice-finding
and a splash of hero worship. She was getting, I joked,
an MFA in How To Write Like Robert Lowell—
you could leave your Allen Ginsberg in your back-
pack on the floor, and keep your Paul Blackburn and
Ted Berrigan, those mangy shepherds, outside the door.
I wasn't bitter though. The winter passed like wine
in a rectory and the Arab spring played out in my dreams
if only I knew all that it meant would be happening.
I burned peas on the stove and my tongue on pizza
on alternating nights, but I was kicking ass
compared to Moammar Gadhafi. My cinéma vérité
was accurate as could be. Every word I wrote down
was absolutely true, metaphorically. And when
I read the major poets like Ange Mlinko, Katy Lederer,
and Kristin Prevallet, I earned their deepest confidence
(my girlfriend sometimes got jealous). They let me know

their favorite scented candles and/or TV shows
and gave me permission to ruminate all evening
on the concupiscence of snow angels. Like Paradise Lost
the twentieth century had been so "object-oriented,"
I hoped for the end of checkbox this and drop-down that,
I hoped for carbon-neutral living with a Jazz Age feel,
I hoped for acoustic punk concertos and intuitive collage
and a fix for the exponential informational cascade,
but the muse stopped calling. I wanted to get paid,
so I commuted against the sky each day. The highway
hummed like microwave rice and my car smelled
like scab. Barbarous collar. Eventually I found it
impossible to modify nouns with unlikely adjectives.
My tongue flitted about like a scarf in the wind;
I coughed more than I thought. My exquisite corpse
would be cremated one day, my ashes scattered
in an abandoned construction site after my future wife
forgot them beside the car at the restaurant where
my friends and family adjourned, and nothing I could do
would make that matter at all. The proboscis
in my arm—expecting me to yield—that was the day
I walked into the woods with no shirt on and screamed
at the chirps, the leaves, the ticks I couldn't see.
I wanted to embrace the future. I wanted to move
to a new town, to a new home with the woman
I loved, and I wanted to direct a micro-budget film
about a girl who runs away from her abusive father
and negligent mother and hides out in the woods
by the river with a cinnamon bad boy in an astronaut suit
to the tune of "Pink ribbon scars that never forget."
I couldn't do both. I knelt in the dirt, scooped some
in my hands, and rubbed it over my chest. I shut

my eyes to the light, counted mosquitoes in my mind,
and when I got to a hundred I opened my eyes,
twitched my nose, and hopped out onto the grass
where a cold drop plopped down from the sky
and surprised my fur like some mysterious sound.

ON MEETING ROBERT CREELEY

I walked in circles more like figure eights
crisscrossing the streets in and around
Kendall Square and MIT—it's not like,
having lived in Somerville for a year,
I was a stranger to Cambridge—but
I couldn't find his reading that evening
the way I couldn't land a better job than
Lead Inventory Clerk at Borders Boston.
The humid air was nothing compared
to the misery of missing what I came for.
Like an abandoned guitar case, I sat
on a bench for an hour and a half outside
the Au Bon Pain, unsure what to do, not
wanting to go back home to the apartment
to my girlfriend who was ready to kick me
out for breaking my hand against the wall,
for shouting at the fridge for being empty
and the books on my shelves for sitting
there, mocking me, making me sneeze,
and for wanting nothing but sex and food
and time enough to hurl my body into
the sheetrock substitute for the fire field
of poetry. And then I saw him across
the street. I made my way over and told him
I had hoped to catch him read but couldn't
find my way. He shook his head and smiled,
then suggested we duck into BeanTowne
Coffee House, grab a cup, and chat a bit.
He told me how he "never forgot Williams'
contention that 'the poet thinks with his poem,

in that lies his thought, and that in itself
is the profundity.'" I protested when he
forbade me to pick up the tab, his fingers
landing on mine like a rain which lets you
know not to go. "Kindness is beauty,"
he said, "and that's the truth. The one thing
we need to remember. That our words
be the pieces to the world we amount to."
And before we stood up to pop the road
in the nose, I recited a short work of my own,
which I carried in my head, about riding the T
with a name tag on and reading what other
passengers were reading while I held The Cities
by Paul Blackburn with its blue cover in
my one good hand. I spiraled out of my head
and the roof through the rafters when after
a pause he called it a candle with just
enough light to illumine the room within
the room we were sitting in that night.

SWINGING LULLABY

beginning with a line by Andrei Codrescu

The aggression of health is badly understood
at the beginning of any century, another day,
another hundred pushups, a belligerent crusade
in solitude, crunch and lunge and jog in place,
sit up and fly, lift and curl, back row or gazelle
into a swinging lullaby, a shadowboxing fiend,
as if the lie didn't begin inside the body's tamper-
resistant microprocessors: the barnyard swoon,
the brickhouse jump, the raison d'être stomp—
be that burning tiger in the exercising eye,
don't cramp my trustful reverie: it's just the lie
in anything, bright blue padding to break the fall,
oh, let's make this personal. I believe in the açaí
of intimacy and the celery of taking pains
to tell the ones you love you want them bending
backwards, arching saintly. One is completeness,
the other, finality. To be that blood pressure
dynamo, to be that amber-gold billowing, to be
the wind screams, the candle hands, the glancing
blow originally known as a phantom hit, to bite
down the shoulder, the ribcage, the neck, to rub
the small of the back with cheek and tongue,
to open, to close, and to take the drum down from
its place on top of the bookcase for future children
who can't even on tippytoes quite yet reach it,
those healthy turnips, those legsmacking jamboree-
loving, tower-racing timebombs of tomorrow.
To breathe is to levitate as to live is to swallow

and to take one by the hand is to launch an attack
like a broad spectrum antibiotic, Levaquin flesh
bone and blood, a neuron's constant instant
messaging capability, an urgent inquiry
to the offshored body, *What happened? What was
that? What else to do?* Scattered nutshells,
obscure space, love finds us in The Butterfly Café,
daring us to order the peach yogurt smoothie
as we shift like pronouns under avocado breath,
a conspicuous sense of self so hard to shake
it's easier to tussle a lion's mane, a hot and noisy
icy reticence *I don't understand*, a walking away
and grinding a tooth and for all intents and purposes
praying at The Gold's Gym Library where the mind
sweats and a tamperproof screw comes loose.

CONCUPISCENT FIRE

1

Fire loves a match head the way dreams
love our skulls when we lay them down
on pillows or sofas or blankets on the floor
in the living room on New Year's Eve
where we're always a couple of twenty-
nothings watching PBS's ten-part documentary
on the history of rock & roll, from its humble
beginnings in the 1950s to Lollapooza
in the '90s. We have our own classic footage,
Starflower. Kiss me against the kitchen counter,
kiss me to the gurgling Keurig brewing
a Caribou K-cup. How concupiscent is that?
Move me like a cannonball. Ignite me
with your tongue. Wrap me in your hair
like the January sun, in your perfume of flames,
that I may bury my skull in your end of days.

2

Fire doesn't love anything and dreams just want
to fuck with us. It doesn't matter where we
sleep or how deep. Holidays are memorable—
so? I'm looking forward to the heyday of
uncreative rock & roll. The way water loves
anything—except when you go to bed
without saying good night to me, it hates that—
proves it's hard to get through school without
a dream, just as it's hard to dream without
being tired. The moon is an open road

so let's ride. Just kidding: you can't get there
from here, snap. Love is a concupiscent itch
that most of the time can't be scratched.
For love, it's best to walk an inconspicuous mile
and leave the huffing and puffing to those
who would rather wag their arms than smile.

ON MEETING JOHN ASHBERY

I met up with him outside Lamont Library
where he had just given a splendid reading
in The Forum Room. This was the spring
of '98. In fact, it was May Day. I had
the day off from work because I managed to
get someone at Borders that week to trade
shifts with me. One of the managers there,
Erin I think her name was, said she had a friend
who had seen Ashbery read once and he
gave the most boring reading and that Ashbery
was even known for it. I told Erin
I hadn't heard that. Anyway, it was the early
evening when KC and I rode the red line
into Harvard Square. We got there early
but the place was already packed. We were
lucky to find two seats together just a few rows
in from the back. I remember KC and I
asking each other who this guy was who did
these great introductions at practically every
reading in the Boston area we went to.
It wasn't until a month later when I met
Joe Torra that I learned that Bill Corbett was
that guy. Anyway, the next time I worked
with Erin, I told her how Ashbery gave
probably the best reading I had ever seen,
how his words were perfectly paced and sounded
and spent, how even his asides about the poems
were brief and humorous. When I caught up
with Ashbery outside, he greeted me cordially.
He was possibly the most dignified person

I had ever met, but he was completely without
a superior air. I'm not one to collect signatures,
so I didn't bring any of the half dozen books
of his I owned. Instead, I tried to ask him a
question about the poem as experience and
what it might mean to incorporate a poetics
based on the experience of experience
where words are crucial informants of said
experience, essential instruments but not
necessarily, or at all really, intrinsic to—
but before I could finish my question he placed
a hand on my shoulder and asked me
to be quiet because the people behind us
were saying something, and he was trying to hear.

NONCHALANCE TERMINAL

The emptiness of any beginning, the way we move
elegiacally, choked up at the thought
of what we were and are destined to be again . . .
do I believe in fate?
                       Abstracted out, fate is easy.
Enter your user name and password, and here
is your password:
We swing like shadows from the cool oscillation of hope,
and we know it's a long way down to the river
where there is so much appreciation for the effort
of voicing our instrumental improvisations
you can hear the dark-eyed junco's quieter song
no problem, the turning of a page,
the setting down of a book. And when it comes
to who is doing these things, we know
we are, but we can't help ourselves. There's no stopping
us, in our frigid shells and concupiscent thoughts,
for we will roll the emptiness into a ball
and roll it down the bank, lickety-splash into the river
and imagine it is spindrift and make quatrains
of our disgruntled smiles, our nonchalant catalogs.

IMPATIENT FOREVER

Mess with me, I'll take your bookmark.
It's not that there's a vast impatience in
my heart, but that it is *my* heart! This
service economy cuts both ways, that's
why we're bleeding. But I'm willing to ring
the register of you. I could count the ways,
but sometimes numbers create boredom.
Is it my duty to be genuine? Is that not
a kingdom of boredom? I understand
grime more than myself, maybe. Oh, rot.
Yes, I'm reluctant. I have slumbering
beasts echoing inside me. So how
am I even possible? The window opens
on a wing. We dance to last forever
or we sing.

APTEROUS DRAGONFLY

I think I understand when you rush things
the ordinary intervals become overwhelming
so I don't have to write day in and day out
but I do anyway. I write the stars and that's
no good I don't have that opinion or friends
"how gay." I felt most at home in the world
in the 1970s, from ages one to six, you can
put a stamp on that envelope and mail it
in like this poem or bicycle ride with me
to the cinnamon river in this vanilla spring
through this desperate small brown town
everybody lives in wondering why there's
not a *rat* in desperate like there is in separate
I maybe should have called it chocolate
but it's too late you can't walk through
the same room twice any more than you can
eat PB&J at a picnic table in the sun with-
out getting thirsty or feel an obligation to
the people who came before you, the good
ones, the dead ones, every time you place
your fingertips on the keys gently poised
to type up something spectacular like
a general attitude things would be better
if you moved to Montana and opened up
a smoothie bar with WiFi and a small selection
of poetry books for reading or for sale. As
I moved through the '80s—or was it the '80s
moved through me?—I came to appreciate
William Bonney more than Jesse James,
thus separating myself, enough at least,

from my father, which is emblematic of
my position here today. It's the same feeling
I get when I'm up on the roof brushing off
snow or scooping leaves from the gutters.
Sure, language can take us somewhere,
but only if we're willing to go. That limitation
is the circle we inhabit, less wind in the sail
than sand in the pail. I don't want to echo
anyone in this, not Wordsworth, not Pound,
would rather strike out on my own California
of sound with mistake-filled flourishes like
apterous dragonflies, useless, ugly, unable
even to hide, uncomfortable communication
cultivated from regolith and subsoil and rabid sky.

GRAVITATIONAL HUM

No fine-tuned teacher, no degree of command,
I am, for all the yellow in the world, a fallen man
whose thoughts have kept him off the ground
or tethered to it, depending on how you want
to view it, whose paradise is restricted
movement with a healthy dose of daffy
etiquette, whose unforgettable vision is
the cosmic footloose Holsteins in the tall grass
of I love you, whose lion's mouth lacks
teeth and lips and rarely moves its tongue,
whose Labrador balls work by amplifying
the available hum voltage from the signals
of alien antennae vibrating in the sunlight,
whose guardian angel trembles in hallways,
parking lots, and malls, any time it's dark,
whose psoriatic skin reciprocates the lime
conditions of the day, whose bones yack
but have no say. But let's say our bodies house
the art we like, our color field hyperstations,
our ambient perambulations or port and starboard
symphonies, our carefully constructed
omnivalence noir, the duende word guitar
that brings us where we already are if only
we had recognized its salient, present features
like tambourine time shaking in our hair as
our stomachs growl into cavernous echoes
like concentric ideas calling us to mud meaning
mud as a verb, to volcano vein meaning ripple
and pull like gravitational waves, to reptile
meaning you're alone with the one you love
the way a couple of atoms kiss into a molecule.

ON MEETING CHARLES WRIGHT

Saturday afternoon in Charlottesville, Virginia,
"The best place to live in the United States."
It's September and the Galileo space probe has indicated
there may be water on one of Jupiter's moons,
but there aren't many left who really know and sing the blues.

It's cool, and the leaves that can almost reach us from their
    branches
scratch against the building behind us. A red-tailed hawk
circles under the cumulus clouds, a scotoma with wings.
What can we say to make a difference regarding The Declaration
of Jihad on the Americans Occupying the Country of the Two
    Sacred Places?

You remind me that "poetry is at least as important for what is
    not said,"
but any water on Europa should have frozen long ago.
It's the aura before a migraine, my Cassandra of the Light.
Let's take a walk into the Blue Ridge Mountains.
Let's make like clouds. I'll bring the water; you bring the sounds.

WHAT I WANTED TO SAY BEFORE

I wanted to say the wind sleeps inside a giant skull,
but that's just silly. I wanted to say
when you touch me on the cheek it makes a sound,
but I could never tell what kind of sound it was.
I wanted to put my arm around you, but you were standing
too far away. I wanted to say "too far away" and not
"on the other side of the room," and so I did.
I wanted to say the window was open like an eye on the world,
but it was not specific enough so I left it out.
I wanted to say I didn't exist—to see what it might feel like.
I wanted to put on heart-shaped sunglasses and drive a
   convertible
like a bombshell up the California coast,
but I burnt my toast and started swearing and broke my hand.
I wanted to say your shoe's untied before you tripped down the
   stairs
in front of your students and cracked your forehead open.
I wanted to say "silent drum," and so I have many times,
but I've not quite gotten it right. I wanted to
be a woman in the shower and a man in the sun,
but I could never be one and was stuck being the other.
I wanted to say language like *La la la loo!*
but my son said it first. I wanted to say something,
anything, right into your mouth, which I thought
would be sexy, but I hiccoughed instead.
I wanted to say there was a dove outside,
but it's the twenty-first century for crying out loud.
I wanted to say let's get more wicker furniture,
not! I always wanted to say "not!" in a poem.
I wanted to swing from the foliage in the moonlight

like all good poets do. I wanted to blackbird
and I wanted to nightfall. I wanted to craft some clouds
at dawn, and I wanted to say don't close the door
I'm right behind you, but I was staring at the ceiling from the
    floor.

CHANCE WORKS

You have a chance to be an artist, one
chance. What do you do? I roll up
my sleeves and scratch my armpits
because it's not getting hot in here, it's
just me in my heavy shirt. Stop sniffling
and blow your nose. All things old are
still old. I stand up to my bootstraps,
only they are not straps, they are lashes.
Mark me, please, I want to see if I grow
anymore. Swelter, sweltered, sweltering,
one big story is the impending storm,
which is all hot with snow like an envelope
threatening to seal us in and mail us
nowhere, the other is the Republicans
bickering on stage, saying things like
"bring back the warrior class" and "I do
a lot of doing." Words make the headlines,
but they don't. A poem simply handles
the unending loop of language and reality
outside, the way the wind has the shadows
of the trees on the invisible ropes of
the square circle of the world. Animal
thoughts, swallowed in the leaves, pages
flip, flipped, flipping, the way Medusa's head
gets all over the place when it sheds.
There are a thousand different ways
to make art, and not enough. A studied
savoir faire and practiced nonchalance,
the enchanted diamond armor that we
craft so that our characters can wear—

a subtle difference not unlike the difference
between "it will cohere" and "throw
your hands in the air and wave 'em
like you just don't care." I see your wild
rhyming couplets and raise you rainwater
droplets. Let's go make Little Anthems
that examine how evolution is a theme.
I'm not going to ask you to trust me, but,
believe me, we began as sensitive
terrestrial mollusks, and now it is easier
to imagine the kingdom of heaven
when spiders surprise us. Wandering eye
of the needle, excuse me, just passing
through. The sky sheds its cloudy skin.
Where one work ends, another begins.

ON MEETING ELIZABETH BISHOP

We met at night not far
from Boston Harbor.
We had just stepped out
of the same restaurant,
a classy joint with a blue
crab snapping at the moon.
She smiled at me when I
introduced myself, and it
made me feel for a moment
like I was back in second
grade at St. Mary's School
standing before a pleased
Sister Ellen as I finished
reciting The Apostle's Creed.
I kissed Ms. Bishop's hand
politely, then asked her
how she was. She said "Fine,
you know, it's always fine."
I praised the evening with
its agreeable breeze,
the perfection of her salt-and-
pepper hair, and the casual
mystery of her verse, but
I didn't comment on her skirt
which looked relatively
tight and surprisingly
appealing on a woman of
her age. It wasn't long
before she had to be going.
We nodded to each other

in careful symmetry.
Then we turned and walked
our separate ways
away from the night with
its seafood smells and its
barges being filled
like memory's dark cells.

EVERYDAY MASTERPIECE

"Make every day your masterpiece," I repeat
to myself as the reporter on NPR quotes the father
of legendary basketball coach John Wooden.
Past Dickinson Park and Liberty Field, I drive
my mud-splashed last-century Civic, window
down as my interior fills with the rough aroma
of the fresh-cut blades blinking wet in the low sun.
Make every masterpiece your own, I think,
like Marcel Duchamp's goateed Mona Lisa
or Anne Sexton's thanatotic Starry Night
or Jim Carroll's amplified People Who Died
or this photograph I saw one time of a nude
man with one hand over his genitals and
the other over his heart, his blond bangs
surfing one side of his brow to the other
as he stood contrapposto on the front of
a shopping cart in a supermarket aisle as if
blown ashore on a fanned-out oversized
clamshell to the dense mass-market approval
of the attendant snack bags and soup cans and
just like that the light turns red because the light
turned green—stubby metal toothbrushes
dangling on dark, electric string—commuting
time's no place for the last twist of the last line
I know. Forgive me. I appropriate because I breathe.
What else could there be? Don't answer me.
Don't watch the sky. Watch the road. The sky's
a kind of road. Never mind those marvelous cuts
of shadow there, easily-dismissed turkey vultures,
circling wordsmiths, trickster gods and goddesses

of passing things, like hey man, that was me
in The Love Song of Jay 'Scooter' Prufrock.
I went to school together. I found the mermaids
most convincing. The days were denim and
the nights were leather. I carried a serrated blade
in the open-air hall that was the wrong side
of town, not even an attendant to an attendant
lord, certainly not one to use the word
trousers, but it was me wandering those littered
streets at two a.m., just passing through,
as undoubtedly someday, O indeterminate
reader, this will be you. And so I say, make
your masterpiece every day, or seize one anyway.

DEAR READER

I am determined to tell you the truth
about something. I don't yet know
what it is. Bold spirit? Not so much.
A moody music is no hard target,
but I wanted to be free from words.
We are subject to the stars, always
imagining limits and no limits alike.
The rickety mind, sunny side up
in cooktop time. Feel, burn, and stay
in a corner. Silver petals, 40,000
years, an octopus suffers no fools—
these things are not secrets. We
begin in the early black snow of old
and end, the bees of night around us.

MEDITATIVE CHATTER

Ah, the weather with its recurrent themes,
charming us one minute with clarion sunlight
and luminous birdcall, turning violent the next
as if Old Thunderclaps could burst our eardrums
if she wanted to. When nature speaks we hear
the words we want to hear, all inconspicuous love
and forgiveness, or passionate judgment, or
hazardous indifference. We write the script
and cast the parts and say the movie was already
in production. Look at the rain with its measurable
patter: it's too many pills. How it knows what it is
alone in the crowd, lost and found in the mist
of meditative chatter. ". . . always been miserable
and I don't know why. I never did harm to no one,"
he said. "I know, I know," she replied, patting him
on the knee as he looked out the train window
at the sunlight smirking among the evergreens far
across the pincushion field the way one story ends
another begins. An earthquake is a dreamy seething
zombie army guttering in and out of existence as
they approach consummation—will they seize
our bumpy skulls or blink away in search of other inter-
galactic brains? So it goes. Or else a rust-colored cloud
crawls through town, painting the housing complexes
and single-family homes, the corporate parks and
shopping malls, the banks and places of worship
brown and red, harbinger of the melancholy whirlwind,
the hospital, too. With all due respect to greater minds,
dismissing irony and distance from spiritual revelation
suggests a fundamental misunderstanding of the nature

of things. As our world always was and will be lost,
so poetry is always a ghost of itself, better known
by not being known, that which returns and that which
does not, and so forth. "I think I will go for a swim,"
he said, having not gone for a swim in seventeen years
but having owned a pool for three. A dragonfly
floating on the surface, an iridescent black screw
with wings the shape of blue, prominent identity
opening into an expanded view of infallible process,
the feeling that our time is spent pushing fragments
in and out of place, hoping to get it right or hoping
to free ourselves from the hope of getting it right
with every keystroke the urge to fudge, to skew,
to intervene, to announce *This is who we are*, when
it's readily apparent the sounds form the meaning—
as the weather's mystery remains intact, prescribe
the urge to know to something like the sequential
numbering of rice grains or blades of summer grass
or how the Kalash, Dardic-Vedic descendants of
the fire lances of the Hyperzephyrians, understand
the horned wolves of want, the black water of need,
and the snowcapped peaks of what used to be,
rosy-fingered spawn of Alexander the Great till
the blood-soaked dawn of the Iron Amir, an outpost
of light, the blue centuries of light, bringers of the light
to mountain temples, sun-worshipping winemakers
almost a footnote, surviving in threes. "If it's good
enough for God, it's good enough for me," he said,
walking three job folders to the incoming shelf
in administration, not keeping to himself the secret
he found, though no one wanted to hear it anyway.
To continue walking, right out the front door, into

the yellow wall of the sun, to take that road and stand
among the trees and hear them hashing it out
with the wind, to understand, when it starts to rain,
where the weather report falls short is art's domain.

ON MEETING GREGORY CORSO

The lines in his face
like tiny electric snakes
and when he grinned
nothing happened that
wouldn't otherwise have happened
the setting sun for instance
leaned out of his way.

TO SEE THE WITH THE FAR REMOVED AND SING

Jesus language with its dislocated utterances,
ontological axes, and pivotal, optimistic affirmations,
could there be a more decentralized approach
to the fundamental question of our hyphenated
awareness and established interpretations of
the unilateral variations of the self-extinguishing world
as if something created were nothing more than
something to be siphoned, storied, and destroyed,
such fluid borders, such blind proliferation of discourse
and subsequent geopolitical, economic, and cultural
continental drifts, tectonic shifts, such dominant
tight-knit relationships woven into the sociohistorical
dominion over the subaltern center left holding
the bags of rocks and water and sand, of promised
post-historical land, the sizable dynamics of ants
or bees in amassing their self-identified colonies,
but for our pierced descendants and noble exceptions,
savage mostly, the musician about to sing about
the garden, to unleash that airy or guttural voice
to its mud-splashing, leg-slinging, fur-flapping romp,
to uphold the self-determined roots and let them
dangle in their dirt, to seethe with the intimate
aspirations that break our bones or bring us to
the incremental openings of monumental discoveries,
the limited emergence of first imagined linkages
and realized recognitions, to banish the resulting
overblown, hegemonic claims, to embrace the wings
of the galvanizing and the heart of the far removed.

METAPHYSICAL SKILL SET

The French have a way of winning me over
with their handy metaphysics and subtle minds.
I thought I was reading a prose poem at first
but it was just a series of end-stopped lines
that ran the text measure without turning over.
Nothing is inconsequential, but that doesn't mean
there's a grand scheme, or God, of things.
Metaphysics is a match between the curious
and the bored, sometimes played on a six-string.
The poem can be a mirror or it can be a hammer
striking a mirror and asking you to pick up the pieces,
but I prefer legs and the ephebic *ooh la la*
of the lesbian lizards and psychedelic geckos
found in South Vietnam. When a Snoopy dog runs
it doesn't have to be perfect, it just has to be.
And it's that belief, in the face of nothingness,
that keeps the buskers busking in the subways
rather than bouncing their bones on the third rail.
Not that it has to be that way. Parlez vous francais?
"Not really, but I've translated a handful of poems,
including three quarters of Le bateau ivre—
is that how you say it? I start it off with the line:
Drifting down Rivers that didn't give a fuck.
The contemporary American requires that kick
to keep it real." Nothing is so "unimportant"
that you say "Let it go" without making a conscious
decision to do so. Abraham Lincoln was French
because he was quiet, reserved, and relaxed,
or at least melancholy—you would be, too, if you
were going to be assassinated—and because

he understood the problem and offered a solution
not unlike the dying Zhuge Liang who ordered
his men to make a wooden statue of himself
to dissuade the Cao Wei forces from attacking,
thereby allowing his Shu Han army a safe retreat.
And that's how Lincoln became an honorary
Chinese-American the way Huckleberry Finn
is an honorary Jamaican-American and I'm
an honorary progressive activist who voted
for Nader, whose thoughts were summer lightning,
twice. Fireworks explode in the night—nothing
is actually moving because my jaws are clenching
tight and freedom's just another word for OK—
there must be no religion on at least one planet
with sentient robots and metaphysical play.

ON MEETING CHARLES SIMIC

When we saw each other
in the New Hampshire night
outside after the reading
we smiled in strange
recognition. We both
perked up our ears to hear
the whippoorwills. I went
up to him and we shook
hands, and then he threw
his arm around me, and
like old buds we walked off,
a couple of metaphor's
soldiers—blokes really—in
the Crooked Teeth Brigade.

2

We sat down on a wall
not far from Hamilton
Smith Hall, I believe. We
rolled up our sleeves and got down
to serious talk. He called
poetry the music of chance
and claimed that its secret
desire was to seduce.
I agreed. And then he
gripped my hands and told me,
"Metaphor—blasphemous
angel, eloquent rat—
that's the key. The substance
joining the image seeds."

3

"But what about the poet
whose words are bathed in
the blood of the lamb?
What does he have over
the poet whose words knock
down the soft yellow ducks
at the carnival booth?
And what about the old
wine-drunk professors of
what used to be called
philosophy? What will
they care about father's
scythe and mother's Sunday
skirt? Day-destroying night."

4

Nearing the parking lot
I leaned in and said, "Chaz,
metaphor's nothing but
a nipple to be turned
and twisted just enough
to help reach the sublime."
Honestly, I wanted
to knock him in the teeth
for what he had written
about Robert Creeley,
but reasonable minds
can kick across the ground
together as they stroll
through awful certainty.

THE PROLETARIAT'S END

Printed pages shooting out a pickup truck
spiral down the open road. The eyes
of the bearded man behind the wheel,
all sclera. White noise on the radio,
a fall of lambs fills the afternoon sky.
Roll credits. A riot breaks out in the theater.

ANOTHER DAY COMES HITHER

The days fill with plots like sunshine
I will never understand. Public
water fluoridation has nothing to do
with pouring flour into a reservoir.
I know that much. I may be out-of-sorts,

not to mention off-the-deep-end on
a number of issues, like wanting gun
control, or at least a GPS device
incorporated into every sort of gun,
but I don't have to run for president.

I drink my morning cup of Fog Chaser.
You see, the day hasn't actually
got here yet. It's 6:02 and dark as
climate change outside. The waves
of blue-tinted snow, like small breasts,

like it's my sunken chest that makes me
sing. Not even my wife wants to hear
that. "My purpose is to make my narrative
as truthful as possible." That's what
Custer said. Girl, that's what we are

up against. Suspicious days, long
with truthfulness, yet short on truth.
I feel one coming hither. Coffee gone,
it's time to walk such thoughts away
to where the deer go when it blizzards.

ON MEETING ELAINE EQUI

In her black and white striped shirt, maybe
the same one in her author photo on the back cover
of Decoy which had just come out, and black
jeans, she still looked a bit seventies punk. She sat
in front of the classroom as we pulled ourselves
not so much into a circle as into an amoeba.
She read us a recipe poem by Amy Gerstler
and something about aliens by Jerome Sala,
then asked each of us weekend workshop warriors
to read a poem as well. I read an excerpt from
"Asphodel, That Greeny Flower" and stumbled on
a homonym, but she smiled like she wouldn't judge.
She was interested in fostering discussion and
gave us plenty of space to voice our opinions,
even if one of us said something silly like
"Williams didn't care about rhythm." Later
she asked us to meditate on the importance
of place, and to write our own poems about that
in class. I remembered the basement I wasted
so much time in as a teenager, but I couldn't think
of any place important to me. One student wrote
about his cottage on the Sound. Another wrote
about a secluded spot in the park she frequented
when she was a kid, meaning like a week ago.
I wrote about the clouds. What it meant to walk
in them, to live with them and really get to know
what they were thinking, collecting all that rain.
I hoped Elaine would praise it as a bold concept
bursting with energy and imaginative language
that culminated in nothing less than an unconquerable riff

on what it means to *make* and what it means to *leave
behind*, but all she said was she liked my poem
and I should submit it to Columbia Poetry Review
with a note to say she suggested I send it, and though
I thought that was cool, I also remembered receiving
a note just like that, maybe a year earlier, as part
of a submission to my poetry zine Brass City, and so
I felt like she probably said that to all the girls and boys.

COGNITIVE SLOG

Recalcitrant as the water in Flint,
"Fuck that. We ain't got time to wait
for no email from the nurse."
Dear applause, we are all suspended.
That's why I slather my face

in a bee venom mask and sleep
under its dull stinging sensation
for the pop-up tent of eight hours.
I mean someone has to bring you
the news. Look, there's an empty

beer bottle on the counter and
thirty-seven more under the sink
because ain't nobody got time to
return shit. Some GIF. I go back
to the crisis in Flint. I am deeper

than the water, murky as cake.
Are you feelin' me? "Can you
Sexy Walk like me?" When I hum
"row, row, row your boat
gently down the stream," I am

deliberately emphasizing what comes
next, what comes after the hard-
to-pass anti-corruption legislation
we table and untable in the congress
of ourselves. Namaste and Nae Nae

and if not now then when may
my nobody be excused?

UNMENDABLE GUITAR STRING THEORY

There are people who are not workers?
Oh, I want to be one. Let me have a taste

of that spinach. We are heroic couplets
when we march side-by-side in a parade?

But even standing on the sidelines next
to the Gatorade, the sun gets in our eyes.

Yes, that's where the sun stands. Visible
grammar, that which breaks in our hard-

count songs, each of us trying to draw the other
offsides, that which means "I can't go on,

I'll go on." Impressive groove to pregnant
pause. Unmendable guitar string of stop.

Compulsory mistakes, language of quirk.
We are done playing now get back to work.

ON MEETING ALLEN GINSBERG

First, it was on the telephone. I met him
on the telephone, and it was like just
a phone conversation, and it was, like,
you know . . . Walt Whitman is on the phone!
And then I went to New York at one point,
and I was reading the 211th Chorus from
Mexico City Blues, and yeah, and out of
the corner of my eye, there was this figure,
and I knew right away it was Ginsberg,
and we took a break, and, you know, we
were introduced, and we were talking, and he
was really really sweet, really sweet, really
funny, and I was of course all—*wuh, wuh,
wuh*—and he started telling me how Jack
would have read the piece, and it didn't
take much to understand he was trying
to change the way I was reading, so I
just kind of, you know—here you are, you're
staring at this, one of the most important
poets of the twentieth century, or any time,
and you're faced with the situation like "hey,
I understand what you're saying, and I respect
you immensely, but I'm not interpreting
the piece as Jack or you, I'm reading it as
me, so it's kind of my deal at the moment,"
and it was one of the most difficult things
I've ever had to say to anyone, and he was
great about it. He was kind of, "Oh, I see,
okay," and I remember I had a cigarette
and I lit it up, and, smoking the cigarette

I remembered his "don't smoke" chant, and
it was like "oh god!" you know, stepping in
shit, one foot after another, it was like a long
pile of shit. Then we went to his place and he
asked me up for tea. I went up and had a tea
and we sat there and spoke about Kerouac
and Burroughs and the early days, which was
a dream come true. And one of the kinder,
sweeter, sort of more beautiful gestures,
he said, we were in his kitchen, and he said,
"You want to smoke, don't you?" and I said,
on the verge of nicotine seizure, "Yes, I do."
He said "Well, you can smoke, but you'll
have to sit by the window," so I reversed
sides and opened a window and sat there
and smoked, and he took a picture of me.

MYSTERIOUS SHIBBOLETH

Nothing says tears like laughter, that's
what I always say. Do you believe
the opposite is almost as convincing
around the body and tucked at the waist,
a cover for living tissue or a structure
for the blade of a knife or sword, but
who carries swords anymore, am I
right? Unless you're some kind of terrorist
hoping to make a point, or a virgin
done with Shirley Temples and getting
serious about self-protection. The second
amendment is a vast and ordinary cow.
I wouldn't say sacred. Let me make you
a shibboleth. No, no, that's not the
right book. You need the master book.
What, you don't have the master book?
It's 1:14, and I don't know, a.m. or p.m
I had the craziest dream. We were sloshing
through Bethel, not far from the home
you grew up in, and you turned to me
and said, "I thought you were done with
narrative?" and I was like "Do I look like
an ear of corn?" and that's what you were,
and all I could do was laugh daggers
in my guts as sunshine wet my cheeks,
and would you believe no one's ever
said that before? True dat, pookie.

MYSTERIOUS OPPONENTS

Be prepared to roll up your sleeves
and fail. Be an envoy who says little
but thinks big. Be a national wildlife
refuge—no, be an international one.
Joss will be at the house at 5:30.
I know it's a pain for you to drive over
during commuter time. We'll go early
so kids can swim. Coins at the bottom
of the pool are brighter, no?
All of the companions, formally introduced
like starfish at the marina—remember
to smile, won't you? I don't want to be
a cruel wind, just want us to be prepared.
A few extra words are fine, just don't
snowball down that hill. They live up
there with their okey-doke Labradors.
You can get more specific directions,
but basically, it's roll up your sleeves:
Take 7 to 35, 35 to Cedar, Cedar
to Deer Hill. House is at the end.
The street signs might be hard to see.

CAMBIAL MIRROR

New branches on an old tree, the reductive
conformity of seasons, of change. A parrot,
for instance, has a large, thick tongue
like somebody tell me what this totem means.
Just because love is arbitrary doesn't mean
it's not deep, as I imagine I must be inside
my catenary love. I am staring at the back
of a tree like a great horned owl with his head
turned around. Cambial mirror. A laugh of lilac
rubs against my nostril hair. I see what I'm saying
now, calcium carbonate and sucrose in citrus
colors with the theme song from Cheers stuck
in reverse in my head and my mouth crunching
the chewable grab anything wandering
around in the barbules of the trees and the tops
pointing thataway, west I guess, in the steadily rising
Orphic wind. A nutshell falls, green helicopters
twirl, shoots and suckers mar the old growth
with hope, with pointed dreams, with new ideas
brandishing the blades of permanent change
as if that wouldn't be exactly the same.

ON MEETING DONALD HALL

He talked about the Blue Mountains
as the opposite of growing old,
and how the white apples of going on
taste, at first, like stone.
He discussed losing everything
as the most human accomplishment,
and I wasn't sure if he couldn't be
more right or more wrong.

CHANGELING COMPLEX

We are now believed, within ourselves,
to be more mature than once we were,
for instance, this stalled language
abbreviates the sublime intentionally,
in case you didn't know. For now that we
are older, we are knowing more. There,
there. What? I shall bestow my award
upon you. The humdrum of freedom
is yours. No more the O of pigeonholed,
you are free to O and be swept away
by the dedicatory broom of contemplation
of the small hours, that narrative build,
the programmatic iterations of impending
evenings, mornings, and afternoons,
you know. The useful tug of willingness
and feet on the ottoman staring out
the window open on a wide white wing.
The way a fact takes a mirror, the shape
of a mouth is abstraction's bold shape,
and you embark on your Stevensian walk
with your headfirst swagger into the world
of headfirst art. Free to walk the rhythmic line
of the sea's easy stars, no wrong thoughts,
no "doesn't appear that way." Actual self-
knowing is less metaphysical tension
and more beautiful impulse like dancing
with mannequins in a dusty attic or empty
department store. The hollowed out shell
of some skin. Slip me the words "always"
and "never." Yes, your mind is constantly

on fire, each of your penetrating thoughts
cocks your neck, the way a fist gets slung
when it's swung. I'll meet you halfway in
the difficult burlesque of Destroy It All.
Fleeting? That's my middle name. I am
the lungs' last overwhelmed plea—home
to breathe, breathe, and breathe finally
and finally to breathe, why we go, alone.

GUNG-HO CONTINGENCY PLAN

Scrambled hair and kung fu eggs, I stand
inside the gung-ho winter morning sun.
When it succumbs to the guttural rain
the devil takes off his shirt and grabs his wife
by the hair. But I am thinking of another woman
whose consistently stockinged toes land in
my thighs whenever I close my eyes.
The mind, with its accelerated cost
recovery systems and calendar effects,
requires such contingency plans, no?
The cross elasticity of demand
collaborates with sordid dual distribution
avenues. One's inventory turns—
even the guttural rain could be the jobber
pitching the ideas to increase your market
share. Net Present Value. Not Invented
Here. Product Life Cycle. Love, like breakfast,
is profit before interest and taxes—
when I cup those stockinged feet in hand
and thumb them up and down, it's less a sales
forecast than a disaster recovery plan.

NIGHT SONG

Lifting the covers, I slide my body over yours.
I am a wretched beast you cannot see.
Our love is sharp and multifaceted, won-
drous as a garbage disposal to the ears of a child.
You tip me over, and the rind of me
rips into so many pieces of woah and yes.

HELLACIOUS EVERGREEN

beginning with a line by Lou Reed

"I'm not a young man anymore." I've got nothing
on my grasshopper mind all the pollen time
like when I was young. I'm speeding along in
my black Civic remembering my trouser-brown Pinto
could barely make it up green '70s hills.
My heart is an eight-track. It's A Star Is Born
every time you sunshine in, or out, the door.
The woman in the crow, that's what you are,
Queen Bee. Lost inside Hellacious Acres,
crippled moon, I believe with one more "Watch
closely now" you'll be the evergreen I turn to
when I look out the window in winter and think
Reprise everything but "The Black Angel's
Death Song." Let me pull into the gravel driveway
of English muffins and eggs over hard. Let me
be your animal Droid auto-correcting its name
to Druid. Let "Shut up and respect me" be
our legacy as we writhe in our bed like bacon
and steam with an ecstasy like grasshopper ice cream.

GREATER THAN GONE

Harder than diamond, faster than light—
no, there won't be time. Brown leaves
across the ground, we rustle when we walk
but nobody will have been singing about us.
What does our battered, twine-tied mailbox
in its constant quotidian fight to remain
hold today? The sun is a sloppy, yellow oatmeal
but so much more. There won't be time.
Let me loafe like bread while I submit my work
to Noon and wait and hope for acceptance.
Let my keel burst, and let my charges climb—
when you're not here, all I am is paper and pen.
Yellow-bellied chamomile, so much blue to contemplate—
shit, we're late. It's true. There won't be time.

ON MEETING LOUISE GLÜCK

It was a Monday in April in '97, a couple of nights
after the Saturday night that Kreg and I were working
at Harmon Homes in Danbury and heard that Allen
Ginsberg had died and we sat at our desks awhile
not proofing the ads we were supposed to be proofing
but reminiscing about Allen's awful singing, O Rose
thou art sick, and how beautiful it was. I remember
it was Monday because I remember my schedule and
I was covering that night for Nicole who wanted to hear
Glück read at UConn as part of the Wallace Stevens
Poetry Program. Kreg had the night off and chauffeured
Nicole and KC, my girlfriend of more than a year,
to Storrs while I proofread real estate ads and fielded
jokes from my coworkers—and boss!—about Kreg
being alone with two attractive young ladies, *ooh la la*.
I laughed and went along with the jokes even though
the jokes weren't funny because if I objected at all
my coworkers would think I was really concerned
and I wasn't concerned, plus I didn't want to be seen
as a party pooper pontificating on our patriarchal society
and the latent sexism in our popular understandings
of gender roles and the sexualization of fucking everything.
Around eleven o'clock KC called from a pay phone
and told me they hit a hunk of metal or something in
the middle of the highway and it shredded two tires
so they had to walk a few miles to the nearest exit
and find a gas station and have the car towed; they were
past the Bucknell Mall off, she thought, exit 62,
and now they were shivering, calling from the pay phone
with their only quarter, and could I get out early to pick

them up? After I took more razzing from the crew
about the old broken-down car trick, *wink wink*,
my boss let me punch out so I could save the day.
I made great time, under an hour, and found my friends
sitting on a curb at the gas station. They climbed into
my Stanza, for real my first car was a Nissan Stanza,
and though their night ended rough, they said it was
fun, even Kreg, who was more of a Bukowski guy. I
don't remember their good time details, focused as
I was on watching the road with my already spotty
night vision, but I know KC picked up The Wild Iris,
which she had Glück sign, and Nicole gave me
Proofs and Theories as a thank you, though possibly
that was an earlier gift for something else, like
Christmas, but I remember reading it and being
pleasantly surprised to find an essay on George Oppen
and thinking of Kreg and Nicole as wild deer
wending away in that goodbye gait that people get.
Later that year, KC, Nicole, and I, having made the move
to Somerville, Mass, went to see Jorie Graham read
at Harvard's Lamont Library and we overheard
a woman sitting across from us tell her friend, "That's
Louise Glück." I could have seen which woman the woman
was pointing to in the audience, but I didn't follow
her finger; instead, I closed my eyes, I can't believe
I'm saying this, and pictured Glück as she appeared
in her photo in The Young American Poets
in 1968, and I thought exactly how, if only
I had been alive—and we had a mutual acquaintance
or friend—I would have liked to have met her then.

ONLY AIR

beginning with a line by Maxine Kumin

Hauled into the office, muzzled, and then
the struggles of imagination begin.
You see there's no such thing as a long life.
You keep a piece of paper in your pocket,
but reaching for a pen, you grab air.
The sunlight is only another kind of water
you have to leave your desk to drink.

THE ARTICULATED BRIDGE OF NOW

The past provokes inescapable clutter,
a tune, a scent, an Allen wrench. In
the middle of beyond, a few blue pixels
void the land. Pylons light the hills.
The early moments of the day, an echo
of weight, we cross the sky methodically
on the struts and wires of our thoughts,
an homage to the haphazard faiths
of the past into the vague kaleidoscope
of the future in all of its precious absence.

NIGHTBROKE

Let's pretend some things are not arbitrary.
The nosy owl, the smeared scent of white pines
bordering the yard, the yellow Colonial
barely lit up inside, one window visible
on the first floor, showing a lamp, a plant,
and a patch of orange wall, one window on
the second, showing a blank rectangle of space,
each its own mini-stage or screen that revives
each time a silhouette enters and stars
within its frames, whether to search a drawer
for some lost tool, as if the night could end
under repair, or merely to step forward
and look, not out, but into the blunt glare
and, after that mind-fought moment, shut the blinds.

PHENOMENOLOGICAL DEXTERITY

A penny for my narrative, my sweet callus
yo? I've never seen Mean Girls, but I hate
your heathen beard. Tin rill. So much of what
we do is captured in the landscape. I think
and the leaves fall. My love is a longshore-
man's love, awkward as an aardvark. Oh,
lose the attitude, Jon Bon Jovi. The people
in this poem are no mere characters, we
are pieces of my heart, river-crossing tokens.
We shovel pain like misshapen mouthfuls
of penne alla vodka, wondering *Where did
Dave Chappelle go? Where did "Rock the
Casbah" go? Where did all that asbestos go?*
Look, there's a notornis in that violet and
there's dough in that postage stamp, baby.
Perturbed snack. I mean, you don't yell fire
in a violet, and you don't be mean. Be dizzy,
be new, be tongue, be cross if you have to,
but don't be a sore narrator. I sweep the leaves
thinking *Do more*. Such praetorian snippets
are so much of what we do. Stop, and then
begin. But you say "Stop or I'll tweet," and then
you do: "It is over, four leaf clover." You love
to roast me, but I refuse to ask for guidance.
You think my earlock's a joke? Who do you
think you are? Texas? You forgot your teeth.
You, who thought Twins was a decent movie.
There's too much oregano in my marinara
and too much Ted Williams in your love.
If you're a piece of me, count your blessings.

My moat is real. Forget what happens, happens.
I hate your beard and I hate your token pain.
I am a violet, you are a fire, and we are a tradition.
I refuse to joke around in your dizzy landscape.
I mean it. I refuse to cross into your Action Park.
So much of what we do is change, but I've never
seen a notornis rock a four-leaf clover, so
goodnight, Texas. I am going to open a spa
in Roanoke, Virginia, where The Food Network
promises to massage the bad stew from my back.

ON MEETING TED BERRIGAN

The way every day is holy sneakers, a shower
of sunlight, insistent hum of cars around corners
and contagious amazement, Ted, swallowing a little
Pepsi with his pills, gulped and said, "Only you
can write your poems, but who hasn't felt the sun
shining on his face through the bedroom window,
waking up with cotton love like a structured form
of remembrance, taken like a cheeseburger
in thoughtless contemplation of the moment?"
I nodded. "Now, that little something on the side
of your mouth, that bit of hamburger juice, that's
your poem. Go get it, genius." And we laughed.
"What else can we do?" he continued, "The sun
has been shining us for a long Whitmanic time!"
With that and a "Terrific!" he stood up and I felt
like a child in the shadow of the Statue of Liberty.
A Buick Century with Paul McCartney and Wings
drove by singing "My heart is like a wheel, let me
roll it to you." Ted lifted an eyebrow and curled
his lips. "It's fun to imagine the sun is mooning us,
that intention exists without us." A breeze shuttled
a pair of ragged leaves across the sidewalk as we
moseyed away from St. Mark's Place. "Be a full-time
hero. A full-time thief of fireworks. Don't put things
off for five years." I put a ten in his hand and we both
said "Thanks, man" and then "Jinx, you owe me
a beer." At the corner where he went left and I went
right, he tilted his head back, face to the sky—
"It's friendlier," he said, "than originally designed."

WAHOO SUNSET

We know the dark side of the sun. In fact,
like the back of a Stratocaster slung low
to rest against a blue-jeaned thigh, it is felt,
the way a crab feels the tide or construction paper
feels a magic marker. Driving the interstate
toward you, wahoo lake in the sky—I want only
to wrap my car around your telephone pole,
no brakes, no airbag, no seat belt on,
the way the aluminum zirconium clouds
rub the hairy curvatures of the earth
to dry the overwhelming question from
our minds, "as if," the way a nasal spray
helps me breathe, puts my body back in place
like *Hey now*, I think you know what I mean.
It's 6:53 in Hollywood, Connecticut, but I
never put down my cold incendiary desire
to smash every mirror in which I appear
without you, the one I love, standing beside me.
Point of fact: We don't know the luminous ball
of burning gas, no matter how many NASA craft
we launch into orbit to photoshoot its stormy
pantomimes. Love, if you can hear me, meet me
at that dark point of departure where we end
and begin, for both are grace. It's nice to know
there's an excess of meaning in the world
the way we flower our brick when we seed.
"Hey, it's a bird," the mother says. "It's a person
dressed as a bird," her seven year old replies,
and just like that, as simple and bewildering
as osmosis, we finger-cross into the future

and we look back at our tawdry selves, fringed
with nostalgia, green around the edges, harsh
and smiling and leaning over the fountain
at a festival in the park where the voices drift
like pine needles, layering the wet ground.
Don't step in the mud, but we step in the mud
out of sheer delinquency or core forgetfulness.
The wandering spider of I think you know—
late gossamer sunshine, let me pass through,
let Scott Christopher Keeney move into
that opposite earth on the dark side of the sun
where he will be a better, more thoughtful and
willing-to-act-on-it soul. Love, my sloe-eyed nucleosynthesis,
be the doe slowly approaching to lick the lake
and break the spell of the clouds *in excelsis*
until wahoo sunset, burning bush on high,
a bare-knuckled feeling from the sun's dark side
clocks us like a clothesline from the turnbuckle sky.

STANDING IN A CORNER OF THE SKY

Where did I leave off? Heels in hand,
but not forlorn. I could break shit:
water glass, dinner plate, Johnny Mathis.
A broken record is a broken heart
is not a sentimental thing to say.
It's a sophisticated day, as alien as
poetry may seem. It's etymologically
true. Where was I going? I could stand
and shout in my parti-colored hat,
but obviously this is going nowhere.
I search myself. I have been the children
wrapped in insightful blanket statements
who do not see everything, but who
seem to see more than I can see. Post-
bond. All that can be reproduced is me.
A public presence like the city abhors,
and I cannot blame. It's a sophisticated
biology that laughs and escapes
but never gets away. Cunning privacy,
normative visibility. Yes, I am crucial
to what I think; that's no secret superbear
but a political position in this ironclad
kingdom of not. The opposite of words
is the real work, unfolds the real news.
Empty space. Revolutions are not new.
And we are not without complicity when
the facts purr into our insurgent ears,
"I will manipulate you. I will dense fog you."

IN THE MIDDLE OF THE SEA
A MIRROR ON THE WALL

Goodbye super-difficult admiration of zero.
Goodbye merely empathetic industry. Goodbye
fundamental moment of romantic equipage.
I think I will be rafting now. I think I will
be relieved of forgettable text. I don't mean
that. My dereliction of love is the tell of life,
the way I say I will not participate, but then
I am participating. Have you seen my words
weightless matter. I make a shipwreck of
any feeling. My glands are walruses. I am
kept in the stockyard of another person
I keep inside myself. My diagnosis happens.
A dislocation of trust is imminent in the exchange
of any lyric memory. Are you feeling me,
cattle prod? I don't mean that. Some claim
to want specifics. I claim this broken hat.

IN THE MIDDLE OF THE MIRROR
A SEA ON THE WALL

To want specifics. I claim this broken hat.
Cattle prod. I don't mean that. Some claim
no lyric memory. Are you feeling me?
A dislocation of trust is imminent in the exchange
I keep inside myself. My diagnosis happens
to be kept in the stockyard of another person's
feelings. My glands are walruses. I am
weightless matter. I make a shipwreck of
I am participating. Have you seen my words,
the way I say I will not participate, but then
I do? My dereliction of love is the tell of life,
be relieved of forgettable text. I don't mean
I think I will be rafting now. I think I will
a fundamental moment of romantic equipage
goodbye. Barely empathetic industry, goodbye.
Goodbye super-difficult admiration of zero.

A POEM FOR DESPISERS OF POETRY

Say you wake up to the blue morning
and you bring your knees up to
your chin as you sit up in your bed
and stare out the window at the sky
you forgot to shut out before turning in
the night before. Say you do this and
the treetops are tilting so that you know
there is a wind of a certain strength
though not so much that it can be heard
through the caulked sill and double pane
glass. Say you consider that silent force
until you feel it strike up/down your back
and it fills your head like nimbus clouds
matriculating into the once clear sky
and the only way the clouds will leave
is to let them rain inside you. Say
you do all this and study the results—
puddles of words, streaks of sound—
only to find an oily, muddy mess with
no way around, but you must get around.

ON MEETING BILL KNOTT

"Poet," he scoffed, as he turned
with the countenance of a sensei
spitting on the floor, then stepped
right through his closed office door.

*

The next time I saw him, he was seated
at the head of a long gray table in a small
gray room. For a while he did nothing
but stare out the window opposite himself,
a block of ice with gray eyes and foggy hair.

*

The last time I heard from him was in
a postcard. It was in response to the copy
of The End Review I had sent him. He said
he wished it were the end of such writing
and that he would like to unsubscribe.
"Bow out," he advised. "Become an apostate."

INEFFABLE MORE

Untamable sand. So many more things to be said.
The dream life of Marcel Duchamp goes on
like slices of bread, winged and wanted.
Unconsecrated day. The dream life goes on
as brothers ride a donkey on the outskirts of Kabul.
They could be Japanese farm boys, or Iowan.
The dream life goes on like the sand in Afghanistan.
The heart is a poppy field, that red in the sun
Shooting hoops, bank shots off the red barn
I couldn't hit the broad side of. Words,
like slices of bread, winged and wanted.
Children, forgive me. I want to be your friend.
The dream life goes on like a cornfield, and off
like a bomb. So many more things that could have been said.

VIDEO GLASS

The way a moment is closer to eternity than a year,
there's silence in the commotion after an explosion—
the dream of a distant land as pointless and ephemeral
as a weekly newspaper. I remember when video tapes
were building blocks. In the current intellectual climate
atheists wake in the middle of the night startled by flags,
a landscape of horses and birds on fire. On my knees,
black hood over my head, I might see things differently.
If the stars came out only one night in a thousand years
over snow globe America, if my teeth were brighter than
they used to be, if the idea of fullness weren't so vacuous
as to undermine the merely positive, we might be free
from the narrative of the supernatural which manifests itself
in explosions and mourning and attempts to counter
What? To jump in the fire of philosophy and pay the bills
on time suggests a certain thrift of imagination, a failure
to find meaning in the submission of self-identification
to gradual loss, which is to say a success, less solace
than threat, in that angelic magic, the idea of it, that wraps
its car around the telephone pole of our consciousness.
But in the burlap dark, one must decide, God or no God,
the relative value of life. That is the authority of physics.
In a cobweb of language, the mind turns; true education
begins on a sleepless night. You dance through the Still River
to a landscape of horses and birds on fire as if by design.
Beautiful accidents, spontaneous violence, nothing exists
apart from quantum instrumentalism that's not abstract.
Entropy. Threnody. Kenosis. My God. To each his own
malaise. Let's go, you, me, and the baby, all the way

to the origin of the species back before the last big crunch. In the Freudian model of yesteryear I'm talking to myselves again. Coffee Coffee BuzzBuzzBuzz. Standby for shrapnel. Often I permit myselves to return to those memory blocks of mine, if only for one throat-clearing moment at a time.

HOW TO COLLAGE

Turn the paper over. Cross the river into fields
or where the trees are performing fall.
Avoid the time of day, or embrace it,
claws and all. Cool the engineered small space
around you. Welcome animal grammar.
The heart holds its own like a violin
just drive at the dawn that assembles and dissolves
The garbage air burns big.
Go home across the river, effortless
and fully dressed. Let things belong together
the way history is its own destination
the way a course is studied, a body shrouded
I did not know where I was seduced by
kinky boots is not a metaphor   I saw some Nirvana

LUMINOUS HUSH

A language is only as beautiful as its grammar
allows it to be a spectacular lantern fish
rising to the surface at night, luminous spots
emitting light from under its consonant scales
as successive powers from a fixed base
form a notational value, an abstract bone,
a public show, the specter of looking, glassed
substantive of keen, frequentative of be.
A language is only as beautiful as its grammar
allows it to be the lights going off in
a yellow house like garden tomatoes as night
drapes the region's window, as bodies shore
their breathing, unsheathing in the dark, as pants
and shirts and words *thwop* the hardwood floor.

DOWN WITH MATTER

Be bitter, I say, it will be ok. Remember the day
we did cocaine in Abraham Lincoln's log cabin:
we couldn't tell if it was morning or night, if we
were kids or just a couple of fucked up adults.
Remember we removed the shelves from the fridge
and you crawled inside for two minutes before
I let you out because it was something we figured
no one had ever done before. Pioneers is what
we were, what we were going to be, painting songs
from the east coast to the west, singing abstract art
to long-haired preppies in ripped jeans and smoked
leather and feather-headed burnouts in alligator
shirts, scribbling poems in the dust that shows up
in diagonal shafts of sunlight. But the sunlight
was just another kind of water, one part present
and two parts not: going and gone. Remember
we swam from the porch to the dock and dropped
ourselves into the lake where we ran like the cops
were chasing us through the woods after we broke
into the liquor store, how we ran across the lake
that night, how we said we would never do that again
so three weeks later we started doing houses.
Be bitter, I say, it will be ok. Remember the day
we could have been so much more, tooting the girls
we teasingly called Muffy and Buffy with Benjamins
in the shiny black attaché of their million-dollar,
Daddy Warbucks Monticello home, taking it in
like catechism, bend by bend and blow by blow,
welcoming the slummers like good slummees.
Remember those scattered moments, suppressing

our anger at the larger world, our lot, our hand,
our inherited repertoire, strumming secondhand
guitars and crooning "A man saw a ball of dirt
and worms, vaginas twinkling in the night, fire-
wing and shiver-hum, decapitated earthlight,
oh oh, oh oh, oh a woe oh oh," etcetera. Now,
a single, large-sail cloud in the sky takes me
to where you are, where you would be if
you were: the water tower, the cross on the hill,
the empty woods behind the shopping center.
Be bitter, I tell myself, it doesn't matter anyway.

THE DAY BEFORE NEW YEAR'S EVE

The ground is not for me with its borrowed fleece
and clouds hovering like taunting children,
with its lumps and depressions and outright holes.
There's no situation here. I'm alive and the light
jangles. Electric light. iMac light. I'm a monkey
at the computer, but a clumsy person at the tree.
I'm New Year's Eve tomorrow and Auld Lang Syne
today. I'm Bobby Burns to my family and
John Brandi to friends and strangers. I'm a scholar
with any knife and a chef with any song.
I've thought a lot about the morning, the way
it comes on like descending smoke, a purple skull,
but my thoughts occur inside a plastic bell,
click-clack until   I know the way a pigeon knows

AS LONG AS GRUBS BLOSSOM

for Hoa Nguyen

Yellow-bellied songbird   sing us a crown
as long as grubs blossom. High leaves
like secrets, cups of beeswax. The green
stop stop of being. I like the squawking too
bird, the no-no shopping spree. I rain
for change, like to see the grazing faces,
chimes of purple light, next door
roaming ghosted buffalo. We kingdom

>people
>rain on rocks
>rocket fuel   and milk
>can hurt

>hurled smiles
>hurtled   apple work
>some
>stabbing   water   useful

>yeah right   why
>history waste
>river?   rapid papers
>fall

>from zombie
>desks   numbers

rage to be a people. One face can want
to picture soul—elegant ripped Wednesdays
gown, a whole mound of pop or mouthful
grass, something fit to barefoot walk on.
A two-bird sonnet in a one-stone world,
big bank sun, getting to be too late to play.

ON MEETING ARAM SAROYAN

dint

OVERBAKED WAHOO

When I paste an illustrated tyrannosaurus rex
into the mountains behind the winding road
of a Lexus ad, I am building a rapport with you.
I am not a raptor and you are not a mackerel.
You could as easily paste me into a landscape
as I could paste you. Inner-city emeralds
scattered across the blacktop, not broken glass
but fog brains. In this way, our collages have
sometimes come true. Like simple words,
like complex ideas—if Wallace Stevens once
walked here—we disappear. Love, actually
is quite small, like a banking account close
to being overdrawn. Love's an invisible drool.
Collage-resistant, love keeps its pieces to itself,
a suicide. The Cults are singing "Go Outside."
That was the year I believed in myself. That
was some shit. There's not a lot I'm proud of.
I clicked Newer Posts, but the same stories
appeared. Trying to read upside down is what
I mean. The effect I'm going for. Let's chew on
the straw of narrative bent between our teeth.
You promise you won't bite me? Be like the sky
and don't hold back. After all, we're pressed
for time. The Cults are singing "Abducted."
Let's paste the huge blue halogen face of the new
flashlight over the moon in the night, to shine
a light on the semi-automatic actions of today.
Log Off. Restart. Shut Down. Fuck You. The way
fog across the ground is everything around
I am a theory and I am a thread. You might
find me derivative; you might not find me at all.

TO FRANK O'HARA

1

I think maybe you weren't writing to
John "A Whistle Blew" Ashbery
but to me because Du Fu and Bai Juyi
were not contemporaries, having
missed each other by a couple of
years the way we missed each other
by a small handful, in which case
maybe you can be Li Bai and I can
be someone whose name was but
a small leaf from history's twig
dropped to earth, disintegrated.

2

When you went like the blossoms
over the windblown grass, do not pass
Go, you were two years younger than
I am today in this century you had
no chance to stroll. Tonight, the moon,
empty as a headlight in the daytime,
loses its bright over the twittering city
as I hear your voice from my inherited
in-need-of-repair antique radio say,
"Funny how the names change
but the people stay, basically the same."

BEGINNING TO END

So the question becomes whether to go on,
why, then how. Whether to play the goon
to archvillain time, to be the mellifluous thug,
the strawman that actually does the attack
and deflects what arguments the sky spouts
with its sun and its moon and its ordinary stars,
with its clockwork of clouds and precipitancy
like what poet is not a poet of the weather?
Stormchasers Inc., through city traffic, bosh.
The exurban weather thickens and relaxes
like a dog on the cloud of an airing-out mudroom
where the boots converse with the melting snow
they tracked inside. I mean, sometimes to talk
is to forgive. Smarmy truth. Here I am, forgiving
myself, legs crossed, trying to forget that I
must go, if not go on, because of how rude
it would be to stand up mid-conversation
in what might be our first meeting, to commit
that "fa paux," to break the unstated oath
that is happening here between us, the way
the winter ocean cajoles the shore, quick
and remindful of that thing we can't quite place.

NONSTOP ENDING

Like a young senator too inexperienced
to be president, I say what I feel
must be said—over and over and over again,
I bring my hard programmatic message,
putting myself on the widening disappearing spot
every time I step out into the dark light
of the stage that is a document's opened page.

Words undergo a transformation into print,
a slow exaggeration of time, and you are with me
in exotic anywhere, but our movements take us
away from each other, away from the longevity
of art sensible as fluorescent shoes at a funeral,
the way answers flee our pestering voices,
questioning one instant, chatting the nonstop next.

MOON SHOT

Moon, don't go upstairs, I have something to say.
Stay a bit among the trees so the birds, despite
shifting personnel, can maintain their commitment
to extreme energy, the way the sun is increasing
violin. Twenty-six crickets and a red fedora set
the tone. In the room where my love and I spot you,
Spanish-fly incense evokes a spot-on characterization
of another dimension where death is conquerable
as a conversation. Look at that river. Feel the physical
bend in the silence. The wealth of bottled water.

Scott Keeney is the author of *Early Returns, Pickpocket Poetica, Walloping Shrug,* and *Sappho Does Hay(na)ku*. His works have appeared in *Columbia Poetry Review, Court Green, New York Quarterly, Poetry East,* and elsewhere. He lives with his family in Connecticut.

www.ingramcontent.com/pod-product-compliance
Lightning Source LLC
Chambersburg PA
CBHW051347040426
42453CB00007B/459